BHAGAVAD GITA TALES

DISCOVERING YOUR TRUE SELF
THROUGH STORY AND SPIRITUALITY

SOURISH DUTTA

To Shri Laxmi and Narayan, the all-pervading God who guides us all on our spiritual journeys, this book is lovingly dedicated. May their infinite wisdom and compassion shine through the pages of this text and inspire all who read it.

To all the Sadhakas and spiritual seekers who yearn for a deeper understanding of the mysteries of the universe, may this book offer you insight, guidance, and inspiration on your path to self-realization.

To all the spiritual Gurus from time immemorial, whose teachings and guidance have illuminated the way for countless seekers, this book is offered as a humble tribute to your eternal wisdom and compassion.

To my mother, who has been a constant source of love, inspiration, and support throughout my life, this book is dedicated with deep gratitude and affection.

And to Madhushree, a dear friend and spiritual companion, who has shared with me the joys and challenges of the spiritual journey, this book is dedicated with heartfelt appreciation.

Finally, to all those who have embarked on the journey of spiritual awakening and seek the wisdom of the Bhagavad Gita, may this book be a guiding light on your path, illuminating the timeless lessons of love, courage, compassion, and inner peace that are at the heart of this sacred text.

Contents

Foreword

It is our great pleasure to introduce this inspiring and insightful collection of stories based on the teachings of the Bhagavad Gita. As co-writers of this foreword, we are honored to have been a part of this beautiful journey of spiritual exploration and discovery.

Through the power of storytelling, the author, Sourish Dutta, has skillfully woven together timeless spiritual principles with engaging and relatable tales that will capture the hearts and minds of readers from all walks of life. These stories are not only enjoyable to read but also offer profound insights and practical wisdom that can be applied in daily life.

As spiritual seekers ourselves, we have long been drawn to the teachings of the Bhagavad Gita and have found in its pages a source of profound guidance and inspiration. We are delighted that this book can now offer that same gift to others.

We would like to express our deepest gratitude to the author for bringing this book to life and for sharing his wisdom and insights with the world. We hope that readers will find in these pages a source of inspiration, guidance, and transformation, and that the wisdom of the Bhagavad Gita will continue to guide and illuminate their spiritual journey.

With warm regards and blessings,
Soma Pal and Madhushree Ghosh

Preface

The Bhagavad Gita is one of the most revered and beloved texts in the world of spirituality and religion. Composed over two thousand years ago, it is a timeless and profound guide to the path of self-realization and inner transformation. Its teachings continue to resonate with spiritual seekers across the globe, offering practical wisdom, inspiration, and guidance on the journey of life.

As a spiritual seeker and student of the Bhagavad Gita, I have long been inspired by its teachings and have sought to share its wisdom with others. In this book, I have endeavored to distill the essential teachings of the Gita into a series of engaging and insightful stories that will inspire and guide readers on their spiritual journey.

The stories in this book draw upon the rich mythology and symbolism of the Gita, weaving together the ancient wisdom of the text with contemporary themes and issues. Each story is a standalone piece, yet collectively they offer a comprehensive overview of the teachings of the Gita, from the nature of the Self to the principles of karma, dharma, and yoga.

It is my hope that this book will serve as a valuable resource and guide for anyone seeking to deepen their spiritual understanding and transform their life. Whether you are a seasoned practitioner or a newcomer to the path of self-discovery, I believe that you will find in these pages a wealth of insights, guidance, and inspiration that will support you on your journey.

It is with deep gratitude and humility that I offer this book to the world, dedicating it to the all-pervading God, Shri Laxmi and Narayan, and to all the spiritual seekers and

Gurus who have dedicated their lives to the path of truth and compassion. I would also like to express my heartfelt appreciation to my mother, whose love and support has been a constant source of strength and inspiration, and to Madhushree, whose companionship on the path of spiritual discovery has been a source of great joy and wisdom.

May the teachings of the Bhagavad Gita continue to guide us all towards the light of truth, love, and inner peace.

Namaste,

Sourish Dutta

CHAPTER ONE

Once upon a time, on the battlefield of Kurukshetra, two armies stood ready to face each other. On one side was the army of the Kuru dynasty, led by the arrogant and ambitious Duryodhana. On the other side was the army of the Pandavas, led by the noble and virtuous Yudhishthira.

The two armies had been preparing for this battle for years, as a long-standing feud between the two families had finally come to a head. The Kuru dynasty, headed by Duryodhana, had usurped the throne from the rightful heirs, the Pandavas. After years of exile and hardship, the Pandavas had returned to claim their rightful place, but the Kuru dynasty refused to relinquish power.

As the armies faced each other on the battlefield, tension was high. The sun beat down mercilessly, and the dust kicked up by the marching soldiers filled the air. Amidst the sounds of trumpets and war cries, the chariot of Arjuna, the greatest warrior among the Pandavas, pulled up to the front lines.

As he surveyed the opposing army, Arjuna felt a sense of despair and confusion. He recognized many of his own relatives and teachers among the Kuru army and felt a deep sense of attachment and compassion towards them. How could he fight against his own kin, even if it meant restoring justice?

Arjuna turned to his charioteer, Krishna, for guidance. And so began the conversation that forms the heart of the Bhagavad Gita, as Krishna imparted his wisdom and teachings to Arjuna, helping him to understand his duty and purpose in life.

Finding Balance: Aryan's Journey of Self-Discovery and Mentorship

Aryan had always been a dedicated and hardworking person. He had grown up with the belief that success came only through hard work and discipline. So, he had always been focused on his studies and his career.

But as he grew older and began to explore his passions and interests, he found himself torn between his duties and his desires. He was an excellent employee at the company he worked for, but he also had a burning passion for photography, which he had never pursued seriously.

Aryan found himself in a state of confusion and inner turmoil. He wasn't sure whether he should follow his heart and pursue his passion for photography or stick to his duties and responsibilities at work. He knew that he couldn't continue living like this and needed some guidance.

One day, Aryan decided to reach out to his friend Mohan. Mohan was an accomplished photographer and had always been supportive of Aryan's interest in photography. When Aryan explained his predicament to Mohan, Mohan could see the pain and confusion in Aryan's eyes.

Mohan listened carefully to Aryan's concerns and then shared his own experience. He told Aryan about how he too had been torn between his passion for photography and his responsibilities towards his family. But he had found a way to strike a balance and pursue both.

Mohan suggested that Aryan should start by exploring his passion for photography on weekends and in his spare time. He could take on small projects and build his portfolio while continuing to do well at his job. Mohan also offered to mentor Aryan and help him improve his skills as a photographer.

Aryan felt a sense of relief and hope after talking to Mohan. He realized that he didn't have to choose between his passions and his duties; he could find a way to pursue both. With Mohan's guidance, Aryan started taking photos on the weekends and soon began to get recognition for his work.

A few months later, Aryan was offered a photography assignment from a renowned magazine. Aryan was overjoyed at the opportunity, and he knew that it wouldn't have been possible without Mohan's guidance and support.

Aryan's story is a testament to the power of friendship and mentorship. With the help of a friend like Mohan, he was able to find a way to pursue his passion and his duties, and in doing so, he found happiness and fulfillment.

Finding Clarity: Raj's Search for Meaning and the Wisdom of the Saint

Raj had always been a successful businessman. He had started his own company and had worked tirelessly to build it into a thriving enterprise. But as he grew older, Raj began to feel a sense of emptiness and dissatisfaction. He couldn't shake the feeling that there was something more to life than just making money.

Raj had always been interested in spirituality and had even dabbled in meditation and yoga. But now, he found himself consumed by the idea of giving up his worldly pursuits and becoming a monk. He was torn between his duty to his company and his desire for spiritual enlightenment.

One day, Raj decided to seek guidance from a saint who lived in a nearby temple. The saint was known for his wisdom and compassion, and Raj hoped that he could help him find the answer he was looking for.

When Raj arrived at the temple, he was greeted by the saint, who welcomed him with open arms. Raj explained his dilemma to the saint, who listened patiently and then shared his own experience.

The saint told Raj that he had also been a successful businessman in his youth, but had given it all up to pursue a life of spiritual devotion. He explained that the path of a monk was not for everyone, and that there was no one-size-fits-all answer to the question of how to live a meaningful life.

The saint then shared a teaching from the Bhagavad Gita, which emphasizes the importance of performing one's duty with detachment from the outcome. He explained that Raj could find fulfillment and purpose in his work, as long as he approached it with the right mindset.

The saint also advised Raj to continue his spiritual practices, but not to view them as a means of escaping his worldly responsibilities. Instead, he should use them as a way to cultivate inner peace and clarity, which would help him to make better decisions and serve his company more effectively.

Raj left the temple feeling uplifted and inspired. He realized that he didn't have to choose between his duty and his spiritual aspirations; he could find a way to integrate both into his life. With the guidance of the saint, Raj was able to reframe his perspective and find a new sense of purpose and meaning in his work.

Following Your Dharma: Isha's Journey of Self-Discovery and Empowerment

Isha had just graduated from college, and she was at a crossroads in her life. Her parents had been urging her to get married and start a family, but Isha had always dreamed of pursuing further studies and becoming an independent woman.

Isha was torn between her duty to her family and her desire for personal fulfillment. She felt overwhelmed and confused, and she didn't know where to turn for guidance.

One day, Isha's best friend, Rhea, came to visit her. Rhea had always been a source of inspiration and support for Isha, and she knew just how to help her friend through this difficult time.

Rhea shared with Isha the teachings of the Bhagavad Gita, which emphasize the importance of following one's own dharma or duty in life. Rhea explained that Isha's duty was not just to her parents or society, but to herself as well.

Rhea encouraged Isha to pursue her dreams of further studies and to not give in to societal pressures to get married. She reminded Isha that she had the right to make her own choices in life and to follow her heart.

As Isha listened to Rhea's words, she began to feel a sense of clarity and purpose. She realized that she didn't have to choose between her family and her dreams; she could find a way to honor both.

Isha decided to have an open and honest conversation with her parents, sharing her aspirations and the path she wished to pursue. To her surprise, her parents understood her point of view and offered their full support.

Isha enrolled in a postgraduate program and worked hard to achieve her academic goals. As she immersed herself in her studies, she found a sense of joy and fulfillment that she had never experienced before.

Through the teachings of the Bhagavad Gita and the support of her friend, Isha was able to find the courage to follow her own path and create a life of purpose and fulfillment.

From Addiction to Self-Control: Amal's Journey of Spiritual Transformation

Amal had always been a good student and a well-behaved son. But as he entered college, he fell in with a bad crowd and started experimenting with drugs and alcohol. His parents tried to warn him of the dangers of addiction, but Amal was too caught up in the thrill of rebellion to listen.

As time went on, Amal's addiction spiraled out of control. He started neglecting his studies and his relationships, and his health began to suffer. He felt lost and hopeless, and he didn't know where to turn for help.

One day, Amal reached out to his childhood friend Basu. Basu had always been a spiritual seeker and had studied the teachings of the Bhagavad Gita. Amal hoped that Basu could offer him some guidance and support.

Basu listened to Amal's story with compassion and understanding. He shared with Amal the teachings of the Bhagavad Gita, which emphasize the importance of self-control and detachment from material desires.

Basu explained to Amal that addiction was a result of being attached to material pleasure and not having control over one's mind and senses. He advised Amal to turn inward and focus on developing his inner strength and discipline.

Basu also shared with Amal the concept of karma yoga, which involves performing one's duties without attachment to the outcome. He encouraged Amal to recommit himself to his studies and to approach them with a sense of detachment from the desire for success or achievement.

With Basu's guidance, Amal began to turn his life around. He gradually weaned himself off of his addictions and began to focus on his studies and his relationships. He learned to find joy in the process of learning and growing, rather than in external achievements or pleasures.

Through the teachings of the Bhagavad Gita and the support of his friend Basu, Amal was able to find a new sense of purpose and direction in his life.

Discovering the Self: Arup's Journey of Self-Realization and Inner Peace

Arup had always felt disconnected from his family. They were harsh and critical towards him, and he often felt like an outsider in his own home. One day, Arup decided to run away and start a new life. He ended up at a railway platform, feeling lost and alone.

As he sat there, a saint approached him and struck up a conversation. The saint could sense Arup's pain and confusion, and he offered him some guidance.

The saint spoke to Arup about the concept of Atman, or the true self, as explained in the Bhagavad Gita. He explained that all living beings are divine souls, and that the ultimate goal of life is to realize one's true nature.

The saint encouraged Arup to enquire within himself and to seek the truth of his own existence. He explained that by understanding the true nature of the self, one can find inner peace and joy, even in the midst of external challenges.

Arup was intrigued by the saint's words, and he began to reflect on his own life and his inner being. He realized that he had been so focused on external circumstances and the opinions of others that he had lost touch with his own true self.

With the saint's guidance, Arup began to practice self-enquiry and meditation. He learned to detach himself from his past and his family's expectations, and to focus on his own spiritual growth and self-realization.

As he delved deeper into his inner being, Arup found a sense of peace and contentment that he had never experienced before. He realized that his true nature was not defined by his family or his external circumstances, but by the divine essence that resides within him.

With the teachings of the Bhagavad Gita and the guidance of the saint, Arup was able to find a new sense of purpose and direction in his life. He learned to find joy and peace within himself, and to live a life of spiritual fulfillment.

The Awakening

Ananya had always been a people-pleaser. She wanted to make everyone happy, and she was willing to sacrifice her own happiness to do so. She spent most of her life living up to the expectations of others, never questioning whether their opinions aligned with her own.

One day, Ananya woke up feeling particularly restless. She couldn't shake the feeling that something was off, but she couldn't put her finger on what it was. She went through the motions of her day, but she couldn't shake the nagging feeling of discontent.

That evening, Ananya took a walk in the park to clear her mind. As she walked, she came across an old woman sitting on a bench. The woman looked up at Ananya and smiled, and Ananya felt drawn to her.

They struck up a conversation, and the old woman told Ananya about her own journey of self-discovery. She spoke of the importance of living authentically and following one's own path, even in the face of opposition or disapproval.

The old woman recommended that Ananya read the Bhagavad Gita, and she gave her a copy to take home. Ananya began to read the holy text, and she was immediately drawn to its teachings.

She learned about the importance of detachment, and of focusing on the inner being rather than the external world. She realized that her people-pleasing tendencies had been holding her back from living a truly fulfilling life.

Ananya began to meditate and reflect on her own inner being. She learned to listen to her own intuition and to follow her own path, even if it meant disappointing others. She found that as she focused on her own growth and happiness, those around her began to find their own fulfillment as well.

Through the teachings of the Bhagavad Gita, Ananya found the courage to live authentically and to follow her own path. She learned to find joy and fulfillment within herself, and to create a life that aligned with her own values and desires.

The Awakening is a story of self-discovery and the power of the Bhagavad Gita to guide us towards our true selves.

The Illusion of Separation

Arun was a successful businessman, but he had always felt a sense of emptiness and disconnectedness. Despite his wealth and accomplishments, he couldn't shake the feeling that something was missing.

One day, Arun stumbled upon a talk by a Advaita Vedanta teacher who spoke about the illusion of separation. The teacher explained that the true nature of reality is non-dual, and that the perceived separation between self and other is just an illusion created by the mind.

Arun was intrigued by this idea and began to explore Advaita Vedanta further. He read texts like the Upanishads and the Bhagavad Gita, and he began to attend satsangs and retreats with Advaita Vedanta teachers.

Through this exploration, Arun came to understand that the perceived separation between himself and the world around him was just an illusion created by his mind. He began to see that everything in the universe was interconnected and interdependent, and that there was no true separation between himself and the world around him.

As Arun deepened his understanding of Advaita Vedanta, he began to experience a profound sense of peace and connectedness. He realized that the emptiness he had been feeling was just a result of his mistaken belief in separation, and that the true nature of reality was non-dual.

Arun began to live his life with a new sense of awareness and interconnectedness. He saw himself as a part of the larger web of existence, rather than a separate individual. He found joy in connecting with others and in serving the world around him, knowing that everything was ultimately connected.

The Illusion of Separation is a story of awakening to the true nature of reality through the teachings of Advaita Vedanta. Through these teachings, Arun was able to overcome the illusion of separation and find a deeper sense of peace and connectedness in his life.

The Power of Devotion

Riya was going through a difficult time in her life. She felt lost and disconnected, and nothing seemed to bring her any joy or meaning. One day, she stumbled upon a Bhakti Yoga gathering and decided to attend.

At the gathering, Riya was introduced to the concepts of Bhakti Yoga. She learned that devotion to a higher power was the key to finding meaning and purpose in life. Through singing and chanting, she was able to tap into the power of devotion and connect with the divine.

As Riya deepened her practice of Bhakti Yoga, she began to experience a profound sense of love and joy. She saw that everything in the world was a manifestation of the divine, and that by connecting with that divine essence, she could find peace and fulfillment in her life.

Riya found that the more she practiced Bhakti Yoga, the more her life began to transform. She found herself feeling more connected to others and to the world around her. She began to see that everything was connected, and that by loving and serving others, she was really serving the divine.

Through her practice of Bhakti Yoga, Riya was able to find a new sense of purpose and meaning in her life. She saw that the power of devotion could transform even the most difficult circumstances into opportunities for growth and connection.

The Power of Devotion is a story of the transformative power of Bhakti Yoga. Through the practice of devotion and connection with the divine, Riya was able to find peace, joy, and meaning in her life, and to transform her challenges into opportunities for growth and connection.

The Path of Devotion

Kiran was a young man who felt lost and disconnected from the world around him. He had tried many different spiritual paths, but none of them seemed to resonate with him. One day, he came across a group of Hare Krishna devotees chanting on the street and decided to join in.

As Kiran chanted the Hare Krishna mantra, he felt a sense of peace and joy that he had never experienced before. He was introduced to the teachings of Bhagavad Gita and the path of devotion to Lord Krishna. He learned that by surrendering to the divine and engaging in devotional service, he could attain true happiness and liberation from the cycle of birth and death.

Kiran began to attend the Hare Krishna temple regularly and engage in devotional service. He found that by chanting the Hare Krishna mantra and serving the devotees, he was able to connect with Lord Krishna and experience the divine love and mercy. He saw that the path of devotion was not just a spiritual practice, but a way of life that brought meaning and purpose to everything he did.

Through his practice of Hare Krishna, Kiran was able to transform his life. He saw that the path of devotion was a way to connect with the divine and with others, and to find true happiness and fulfillment. He learned that by serving others and living a life of devotion, he could attain the ultimate goal of life: love of God.

The Path of Devotion is a story of the transformative power of Hare Krishna. Through the practice of devotion and service to Lord Krishna, Kiran was able to find a sense of purpose and meaning in his life, and to connect with the divine love and mercy.

The Way of Action

Arun was a hardworking man, but he often felt dissatisfied with his life. He had a good job, a loving family, and plenty of material possessions, but he couldn't shake the feeling that something was missing. He began to explore different spiritual paths and eventually came across the teachings of Karma Yoga.

Karma Yoga taught Arun that the key to a fulfilling life was not to renounce action, but to engage in it with the right attitude. By performing his duties without attachment to the results, he could attain true liberation and happiness. He learned that the path of action was not a way to escape from the world, but a way to engage with it fully and to serve others.

Arun began to apply the principles of Karma Yoga in his life. He continued to work hard at his job, but he did so without seeking personal gain or recognition. He focused on serving his colleagues and clients with compassion and kindness, rather than trying to advance his own career. He also became more involved in his community, volunteering his time and resources to help those in need.

Through his practice of Karma Yoga, Arun found that he was able to find a sense of purpose and fulfillment in his life. He realized that the path of action was not just a way to earn a living, but a way to serve others and to contribute to the greater good. He saw that by performing his duties with the right attitude, he could attain true liberation and happiness.

As Arun continued on the path of Karma Yoga, he faced many challenges and obstacles. But he remained steadfast in his commitment to serving others and to performing his duties with the right attitude. Through his struggles, he learned that the key to a successful life was not to avoid difficulty, but to face it with courage and compassion.

The Way of Action is a story of the transformative power of Karma Yoga. Through the practice of action with the right attitude, Arun was able to find a sense of purpose and fulfillment in his life, and to serve others with compassion and kindness. He learned that the path of action was not just a way to earn a living, but a way to attain true liberation and happiness.

The Service of Love

Sarika was a young woman who had always been deeply spiritual, but she struggled to find a path that resonated with her. She had tried meditation, yoga, and various other practices, but she couldn't seem to find the right fit. One day, she came across the teachings of Karma Yoga and was immediately drawn to them.

Karma Yoga taught Sarika that the path to spiritual fulfillment lay not in renunciation, but in the selfless service of others. She learned that by performing her duties with love and devotion, without seeking personal gain or recognition, she could achieve a state of pure consciousness and liberation.

Sarika began to apply the principles of Karma Yoga in her life. She found work at a local hospital, where she worked tirelessly to care for the sick and injured. She saw her work not as a job, but as an opportunity to serve others and to practice selfless service. She treated each patient with love and compassion, no matter their background or condition.

As Sarika continued on the path of Karma Yoga, she faced many challenges. She struggled to balance her work with her personal life, and she faced criticism from some who saw her dedication to service as a waste of time. But she remained steadfast in her commitment to the path of action and the service of others.

Through her practice of Karma Yoga, Sarika found a deep sense of fulfillment and purpose. She realized that the true path to spiritual fulfillment lay not in renunciation, but in the service of love. She saw that by serving others with love and devotion, she could achieve a state of pure consciousness and liberation.

The Service of Love is a story of the transformative power of Karma Yoga. Through the practice of selfless service, Sarika was able to find a path that resonated with her and to achieve a deep sense of fulfillment and purpose. She learned that the service of love was not just a way to help others, but a way to attain true liberation and happiness.

The Quest for Knowledge

Ravi was a young man who had always been deeply curious about the world and its mysteries. He longed to understand the nature of reality and the meaning of existence. He studied philosophy and science, but found that no matter how much he learned, he still felt a sense of emptiness and confusion.

One day, Ravi came across the teachings of Jnana Yoga, the path of knowledge. Jnana Yoga taught him that the true nature of reality could not be known through the senses or the mind, but only through direct experience and the realization of the Self. He learned that the pursuit of knowledge was not just an intellectual exercise, but a spiritual quest for self-realization.

Ravi began to apply the principles of Jnana Yoga in his life. He spent hours in deep meditation, seeking to quiet his mind and to connect with the true Self. He studied the scriptures and the teachings of the great sages, seeking to deepen his understanding of the nature of reality.

As Ravi continued on the path of Jnana Yoga, he faced many challenges. He struggled to overcome his attachment to his ego and his identification with his body and mind. He faced criticism from those who saw his quest for knowledge as a waste of time or a form of escapism.

But Ravi remained steadfast in his pursuit of self-realization. Through his practice of Jnana Yoga, he gradually came to understand the nature of reality and the true nature of the Self. He realized that the ultimate goal of human existence was not material success or pleasure, but the realization of the Self and the attainment of true liberation.

The Quest for Knowledge is a story of the transformative power of Jnana Yoga. Through the pursuit of knowledge and the realization of the Self, Ravi was able to overcome his confusion and emptiness and to achieve a deep sense of spiritual fulfillment. He learned that the true nature of reality could not be known through the mind or the senses, but only through the direct experience of the Self.

The Awakening of Vivekananda

Swami Vivekananda was a great spiritual teacher and philosopher who lived in India in the late 19th century. He was born into a traditional Brahmin family and was raised with a deep respect for the teachings of the Hindu scriptures.

As a young man, Vivekananda was deeply curious about the nature of reality and the purpose of human existence. He studied various philosophies and religions, but found that none of them provided a satisfactory answer to his questions.

One day, Vivekananda came across the teachings of Jnana Yoga, the path of knowledge. He was immediately drawn to the teachings and began to study them with great intensity.

Through his study of Jnana Yoga, Vivekananda came to understand that the true nature of reality could not be known through the mind or the senses, but only through the direct experience of the Self. He realized that the goal of human existence was not to accumulate wealth or power, but to attain self-realization and liberation.

Vivekananda was deeply moved by the teachings of Jnana Yoga and devoted his life to sharing them with others. He traveled throughout India and the world, giving lectures and teachings on the nature of reality and the importance of spiritual practice.

Vivekananda's teachings on Jnana Yoga emphasized the importance of discrimination, detachment, and self-inquiry. He believed that the ultimate goal of human existence was to realize the true Self and to achieve liberation from the cycle of birth and death.

Vivekananda's teachings on Jnana Yoga had a profound impact on the spiritual landscape of India and the world. He inspired countless people to pursue the path of self-realization and to seek the ultimate truth.

The Awakening of Vivekananda is a story of the transformative power of Jnana Yoga. Through his study of the teachings of Jnana Yoga, Vivekananda was able to attain a deep understanding of the nature of reality and the importance of spiritual practice. He devoted his life to sharing these teachings with others, inspiring countless people to pursue the path of self-realization and liberation.

The Illumination of Swami Karpati Maharaj

Swami Karpati Maharaj was a spiritual teacher and philosopher who lived in India in the early 20th century. He was deeply interested in the teachings of Jnana Yoga, the path of knowledge, and dedicated his life to the pursuit of self-realization.

Swami Karpati Maharaj was born into a family of farmers, but from a young age he was drawn to the teachings of the ancient scriptures. He spent many years studying the Upanishads and other philosophical texts, seeking to understand the true nature of reality.

Through his study of Jnana Yoga, Swami Karpati Maharaj came to understand that the true nature of reality was beyond the limitations of the mind and the senses. He realized that the Self was not the body, the mind, or the ego, but the eternal consciousness that underlies all of existence.

Swami Karpati Maharaj devoted his life to the practice of Jnana Yoga, seeking to attain direct experience of the Self. He spent many years in meditation and self-inquiry, striving to transcend the limitations of the mind and to realize the true nature of reality.

Through his practice of Jnana Yoga, Swami Karpati Maharaj attained a state of profound illumination. He realized that the true nature of the Self was beyond all concepts and words, and that it could only be experienced directly through the process of self-inquiry and meditation.

Swami Karpati Maharaj's teachings on Jnana Yoga emphasized the importance of discrimination, detachment, and self-inquiry. He believed that the ultimate goal of human existence was to attain self-realization and to recognize the true nature of the Self.

Swami Karpati Maharaj's teachings on Jnana Yoga had a profound impact on the spiritual landscape of India and the world. He inspired countless people to pursue the path of self-realization and to seek the ultimate truth.

The Illumination of Swami Karpati Maharaj is a story of the transformative power of Jnana Yoga. Through his study and practice of Jnana Yoga, Swami Karpati Maharaj was able to attain a state of profound illumination and to recognize the true nature of the Self. He dedicated his life to sharing these teachings with others, inspiring countless people to pursue the path of self-inquiry and to seek the ultimate truth.

Arjun's Journey: Finding Inner Peace and Purpose Through the Bhagavad Gita

Once upon a time, there was a young prince named Arjun who was next in line to the throne. He had always been a quiet and contemplative boy, and as he grew older, he found himself torn between his duty to lead his kingdom and his desire to live a peaceful life. Arjun had seen the violence and turmoil that often came with being a king, and he feared that he would not be able to maintain his inner peace while ruling his people.

One day, while on a walk in the palace gardens, Arjun stumbled upon a group of scholars who were studying the Bhagavad Gita, an ancient Hindu scripture. Intrigued, he asked them about the book, and they told him that it contained the teachings of Lord Krishna on how to lead a meaningful and purposeful life.

Arjun immediately felt drawn to the book and began reading it. As he delved deeper into its teachings, he realized that the Bhagavad Gita offered him a way to reconcile his duty as a prince with his desire for peace. He learned that a true leader must act with compassion, selflessness, and a sense of duty towards others, and that by doing so, he would be fulfilling his own dharma, or life's purpose.

Arjun was deeply moved by the teachings of the Bhagavad Gita, and he resolved to follow its teachings in his own life. He began to see his duties as a prince not as a burden, but as an opportunity to serve his people and make a positive impact in the world. He worked tirelessly to improve the lives of his subjects, and he did so with a sense of inner peace and contentment that he had never known before.

As the years went by, Arjun became known as one of the greatest kings in the kingdom's history. He had brought peace, prosperity, and happiness to his people, and he had done so while remaining true to the teachings of the Bhagavad Gita. And as he looked back on his life, he knew that he had found the true purpose and meaning that he had been searching for all along.

The Warrior's Enlightenment

The sun was setting on the battlefield, casting a warm golden light on the hills and fields that lay before the warrior, Arjun. But the warmth that the sun brought was the only comfort that Arjun could find in this moment. He had lost his sense of purpose, and he was lost in the maze of his own thoughts.

As he looked across the battlefield, he could see his enemies waiting for him. His heart sank as he thought of the destruction he would cause if he went forward. He did not want to fight, but he could not run away. He was torn between his duty as a warrior and his conscience as a human being.

Just then, Arjun's charioteer, Krishna, spoke up, "Why are you so worried, Arjun? Do not hesitate to fight. You were born to fight this battle. The path of the warrior is one of honor, and you must follow it."

Arjun replied, "Krishna, how can I fight against my own family and friends? What good will come of this bloodshed?"

Krishna smiled and replied, "Arjun, you are not fighting against your family and friends. You are fighting against the forces of evil, and you must fight to protect the righteous. Remember, your duty is to fight, not to worry about the outcome. The outcome is in the hands of the Divine."

Krishna went on to teach Arjun the concepts of dharma, karma, and moksha. He explained the nature of the universe and the role of the individual in it. He showed Arjun that every action has a consequence, and that the Law of Karma is always at work.

As Arjun listened to Krishna's words, his confusion began to disappear, and he found a new sense of purpose. He picked up his bow and arrow, and with renewed confidence, he stepped forward onto the battlefield. He fought with all his might, knowing that he was doing the right thing.

In the end, Arjun emerged victorious, but it was not just a victory over his enemies. It was a victory over his own fears and doubts. He had rediscovered his true self and had found enlightenment through the teachings of the Gita.

The Wisdom Seekers

Four friends, Aarav, Kavya, Rohan, and Tia, all worked at the same company. One day, while having lunch, they discussed a recent project they had been working on. Aarav had suggested to the client to hide some information in their financial report to avoid paying taxes. Kavya and Rohan had gone along with it, but Tia had raised an objection, citing ethical concerns.

The group went their separate ways for the day, but Tia couldn't shake off the discomfort she felt about the situation. She went to a nearby temple to clear her mind, and found a copy of the Bhagavad Gita lying on a bench. She began to read it and felt a sense of calmness and clarity wash over her.

Over the next few days, Tia shared what she had learned with her friends, and together they began to apply the principles of the Gita to their lives. They realized that their actions had consequences, and that they needed to take responsibility for them. They also realized that true success came not from material gain, but from following one's dharma, or life purpose.

Their newfound understanding helped them navigate through various ethical dilemmas they faced, such as whether to cover up a mistake or to admit it, or whether to take a shortcut in a project or to do it the right way. They always chose the ethical and honest path, even if it meant losing a client or taking longer to finish a project.

Their actions did not go unnoticed, and their clients and colleagues began to take notice of their integrity and honesty. Their reputation grew, and their company became known for its ethical practices.

As time passed, the four friends found that not only did their professional lives improve, but their personal lives did as well. They felt a sense of purpose and meaning, and their relationships with their loved ones deepened.

In the end, they realized that the wisdom of the Bhagavad Gita had not only helped them navigate through ethical dilemmas, but had also transformed their lives, bringing them a sense of peace, purpose, and fulfillment.

The Teachings of the Gita

Mr. Sharma was a history teacher at a high school in a small town. He was known for his interesting stories and engaging teaching style, but he was also a firm believer in the importance of discipline and inner peace. He often shared stories from the Bhagavad Gita with his students, hoping to inspire them to lead a balanced and purposeful life.

One day, as he was teaching his class, he noticed that one of his students, Rohan, seemed distracted and uninterested. After the class was over, Mr. Sharma called Rohan to his desk and asked him what was bothering him.

"I don't see the point in all this discipline and inner peace stuff," Rohan said. "I mean, what does it really matter in the grand scheme of things?"

Mr. Sharma smiled and picked up a copy of the Bhagavad Gita from his desk. "Let me tell you a story," he said. "There was once a great warrior named Arjuna, who was facing a terrible dilemma. He was on the battlefield, about to go to war with his own family members, and he was filled with doubt and confusion. He didn't know if he should fight or not, and he felt paralyzed by his emotions."

Rohan listened intently as Mr. Sharma continued the story. "It was then that Lord Krishna appeared to Arjuna and shared with him the wisdom of the Bhagavad Gita. He taught Arjuna the importance of self-discipline and inner peace, and helped him understand that it is our duty to do what is right, even if it is difficult or painful. Arjuna was able to overcome his doubts and fears, and he fought with courage and conviction, knowing that he was doing what was right."

Rohan was fascinated by the story and asked Mr. Sharma more questions about the Gita. They discussed the concept of dharma, or one's duty in life, and the importance of living a life of balance and purpose. Mr. Sharma also shared practical tips for achieving inner peace, such as meditation and self-reflection.

From that day on, Rohan became more interested in the teachings of the Gita and started practicing some of the techniques Mr. Sharma had shared with him. He found that he was able to handle stress and challenges more effectively, and he was able to stay focused on his goals.

As the school year came to an end, Rohan approached Mr. Sharma and thanked him for introducing him to the wisdom of the Gita. "I never realized how important self-discipline and inner peace were," he said. "I feel like I have a better understanding of my place in the world now."

Mr. Sharma smiled and patted Rohan on the back. "I'm glad I could help," he said. "Remember, the teachings of the Gita are not just meant for warriors on the battlefield. They are relevant to all of us, in all aspects of our lives."

Gopal and the Gita

Gopal was a farmer who lived in a small village in India. He had been tilling his land for many years, and had always relied on the rains to water his crops. But this year, there had been no rain for many months, and the ground was dry and cracked. The crops had withered, and Gopal was facing a crisis.

He didn't know what to do. He had tried everything he could think of, but nothing seemed to work. He was running out of money, and he feared that he might lose his farm if he couldn't find a way to make it through the drought.

One day, while he was walking in the fields, feeling despondent, he came across an old man sitting under a tree. The man was reading a small book, and seemed to be lost in thought. Gopal approached him and asked him what he was reading.

"It's the Bhagavad Gita," the old man said. "It's a book of wisdom that has helped me through many difficult times in my life."

Gopal had heard of the Gita, but had never read it. The old man offered to lend him the book, and Gopal accepted gratefully.

As he started reading the Gita, Gopal found that it gave him a sense of peace and inner strength. The teachings of the Gita reminded him that everything in life was impermanent, and that he needed to focus on his duties and not worry about the results. He realized that he had been too attached to the outcome of his farming, and that he needed to let go and do his work without being attached to the results.

With this new mindset, Gopal started working on his farm with renewed vigor. He worked hard, but without any expectation of the outcome. He did everything he could to make his land fertile, but he didn't worry about the rains or the crops.

As he worked, Gopal found that he was no longer anxious or fearful. He had found a sense of inner peace that he had never experienced before. And then, one day, it rained. The rain came down in torrents, and the parched land soaked it up eagerly.

Gopal's crops grew back stronger than ever, and he knew that it was the result of his hard work and detachment. He knew that he had learned a valuable lesson from the Gita, and he felt grateful for the old man who had introduced him to it.

From that day on, Gopal carried the Gita with him wherever he went, and he shared its teachings with anyone who would listen. He knew that the book had given him the strength to overcome his difficulties, and he hoped that it would do the same for others who were struggling.

The Modern Gita

Mira was a devout follower of the Bhagavad Gita, and she tried to instill its values in her children - Raj and Meera. However, she struggled to find a way to make the ancient teachings relevant to their modern lives.

Raj and Meera were like any other children of their age, and they were more interested in their gadgets and social media than the Gita. Mira tried to find a way to make them understand the teachings of the Gita and make them realize the importance of leading a righteous life.

One day, Mira came up with an idea. She decided to relate the teachings of the Gita to their everyday lives. She started to tell them stories of Lord Krishna and how he applied the teachings of the Gita in his life. She explained to them the concepts of karma, selfless action, and detachment, and how they could apply these teachings in their lives.

Raj and Meera slowly began to understand the teachings of the Gita and their relevance in their modern lives. They started to practice self-discipline, selflessness, and detachment. They started to appreciate the beauty of nature and the importance of living in harmony with it.

As they grew up, Raj and Meera became successful professionals, but they never forgot the values of the Gita that their mother had instilled in them. They continued to practice selflessness and detachment, and they lived their lives with the spirit of the Gita.

In the end, Mira felt proud of her children and the way they had embraced the teachings of the Gita. She realized that the values of the Gita were timeless and could be applied in any era, and she felt happy that she had been able to make them relevant to her children's modern lives.

The Profit of Ethics

Ravi was a successful businessman, driven by his ambition for wealth and success. He believed that the key to a successful business was to do whatever it takes to maximize profits, even if it meant compromising on ethics and values. He had built his business empire by cutting corners, deceiving his clients, and exploiting his employees.

But despite his success, Ravi felt a sense of emptiness in his life. He felt like he had lost touch with his values and principles. One day, while browsing through a bookstore, he stumbled upon a copy of the Bhagavad Gita, a book he had heard of but never read before.

As he started to read the Gita, Ravi found himself drawn to its teachings on ethics, duty, and responsibility. He was struck by the idea that success was not just about financial gains, but also about leading a life of integrity and honesty.

Ravi decided to make some changes in his business practices. He began to treat his employees with respect and fairness, and he started to provide better services to his clients. He also started to give back to the community, by supporting charitable causes and initiatives that he believed in.

At first, Ravi's business suffered, as he let go of some of his more profitable but unethical practices. But over time, he began to see the benefits of his new approach. His employees were happier and more productive, and his clients were more loyal and satisfied. His reputation improved, and he gained the respect of his peers and competitors.

Ravi realized that the Gita had taught him a valuable lesson: that success was not just about profits, but also about living a life of purpose and meaning. He had rediscovered his values and principles, and he was proud of the ethical business he had built.

Ravi started to share his newfound wisdom with others, by speaking at business conferences and mentoring young entrepreneurs. He became an advocate for ethical business practices, and his message of balance between profits and principles resonated with many.

The lessons Ravi learned from the Gita had transformed not only his business, but also his life. He had found a new sense of purpose and meaning, and he knew that his success was no longer measured by his bank account, but by the positive impact he had on the world.

Love and Devotion: Lessons from the Gita

Rahul and Neha had been married for just over a year, but their relationship had already hit a rough patch. They both loved each other deeply, but they found themselves constantly arguing and unable to see eye-to-eye on many things.

One day, while browsing through a bookstore, Neha came across a copy of the Bhagavad Gita. Intrigued, she bought it and started reading. As she delved into the teachings of the Gita, she realized that many of the concepts and ideas could be applied to her marriage.

Excited to share what she had learned, Neha suggested to Rahul that they read the Gita together. Rahul was hesitant at first, but he saw how much the Gita was helping Neha and agreed to give it a try.

As they read through the Gita, they were struck by how relevant the ancient teachings were to their modern lives. They realized that their arguments stemmed from a lack of understanding and empathy for each other, and that they needed to cultivate more love and devotion in their relationship.

Through the Gita, they learned that love is not just a feeling, but an action. It requires effort and sacrifice to truly love someone. They also learned that devotion, both to each other and to a higher power, could bring a sense of purpose and meaning to their lives.

Armed with this new knowledge, Rahul and Neha worked to improve their relationship. They made an effort to listen to each other, to communicate more effectively, and to prioritize their relationship over other distractions.

It wasn't easy, but with the help of the Gita, they were able to find harmony and peace in their marriage. They continued to read and study the Gita, finding new lessons and insights along the way.

In the end, they realized that the Gita wasn't just a book, but a way of life. Its teachings had transformed their relationship and helped them to become better people.

The Activists' Guide to Social Justice

In the heart of a bustling city, a group of activists had come together to fight for social justice. They were a diverse group of people, united by a common goal - to create a more just and equitable world.

As they planned their campaigns and protests, they found themselves turning to the teachings of the Bhagavad Gita for guidance. The Gita, an ancient Hindu scripture, offered a roadmap for living a life of purpose and service, and the activists found its lessons to be relevant to their struggle.

One of the activists, a young woman named Priya, had grown up in a Hindu household and had always been drawn to the Gita. She was thrilled to find that her spiritual beliefs could be integrated with her activism, and she soon became a leading voice in the group.

Together, the activists studied the Gita and applied its teachings to their work. They learned about the importance of non-attachment to the fruits of their labor, and how to stay focused on their goals even in the face of adversity. They also learned about the importance of acting with compassion and empathy, even towards their opponents.

Their first campaign was a protest against police brutality. The activists gathered in a public square, holding signs and chanting slogans. But instead of shouting angry slogans, they chanted mantras from the Gita, sending out a message of peace and harmony.

The protest was a success, and the activists continued to use the Gita as a guide for their work. They tackled issues ranging from environmental justice to workers' rights, always keeping the Gita's teachings in mind.

Over time, the group's efforts began to bear fruit. They won important victories, and their work inspired others to join the movement for social justice.

As they celebrated their successes, the activists knew that they had the Gita to thank for their guidance. They had found a way to integrate their spiritual beliefs with their activism, and in doing so, they had become a powerful force for change.

Finding Inner Peace in the Midst of Chaos

Dr. Anjali had always dreamed of becoming a doctor, but now that she had achieved her dream, she found herself struggling with the demands of her profession. She worked long hours, dealing with the stress and pressure of her job every day. She was exhausted and overworked, and she often found it difficult to switch off and relax.

One day, after a particularly grueling shift at the hospital, a colleague recommended that she read the Bhagavad Gita. Dr. Anjali had heard of the ancient Hindu scripture before, but she had never read it. She decided to give it a try.

As she read the Gita, Dr. Anjali found herself drawn to its teachings. The Gita offered a way to find balance and inner peace in the midst of chaos. She learned about the importance of detachment and how to let go of the outcomes of her actions. She also learned about the importance of selfless service and how to approach her work with a sense of devotion.

Dr. Anjali began to integrate the teachings of the Gita into her life. She took time each day to meditate and reflect, and she started to approach her work with a sense of detachment. She focused on doing her best, without worrying about the outcomes of her actions. She also started to practice yoga, which helped her to stay centered and calm.

Over time, Dr. Anjali found that she was less stressed and more at peace. She had developed a sense of inner calm that had eluded her for so long. Her patients noticed the change in her too. They commented on her positive attitude and her ability to stay calm under pressure.

Dr. Anjali continued to use the teachings of the Gita to guide her life and her work. She had found a way to find balance and inner peace, even in the midst of chaos. She had learned that by letting go of the outcomes of her actions and focusing on selfless service, she could find a sense of purpose and fulfillment in her work.

As she reflected on her journey, Dr. Anjali knew that the Gita had been a gift. It had given her the tools she needed to find balance and inner peace, and she would be forever grateful for the wisdom it had imparted.

Journey to Unity

In a far-off land, a group of travelers from different backgrounds and beliefs set out on a journey together. There was Arun, a Hindu businessman; Fatima, a Muslim scholar; James, a Christian teacher; and Maria, an atheist artist. Despite their differences, they shared a common goal - to explore the world and discover new perspectives.

As they traveled together, they encountered many challenges. They faced language barriers, cultural differences, and misunderstandings. They found it difficult to communicate and connect with each other, and tensions began to rise.

One night, as they sat around a campfire, Arun suggested that they read the Bhagavad Gita. He explained that the Gita offered a path to unity, even in the midst of diversity. The others were skeptical at first, but they agreed to give it a try.

As they read the Gita, the travelers found themselves drawn to its teachings. They learned about the importance of finding inner peace, and how to approach life with a sense of detachment. They also learned about the importance of selfless service and how to act with compassion and empathy.

Over time, the group began to apply the teachings of the Gita to their interactions with each other. They learned to listen to each other's perspectives and to approach their differences with an open mind. They found that they had more in common than they had realized, and they began to build connections that transcended their backgrounds and beliefs.

As they continued on their journey, the travelers encountered new challenges, but they faced them together, with a sense of unity and purpose. They found that the Gita had given them a common language and a shared framework for approaching life.

By the end of their journey, the travelers had formed a bond that would last a lifetime. They had discovered that despite their differences, they shared a common humanity, and that by working together, they could achieve great things.

As they said their goodbyes, the travelers knew that they had been forever changed by their journey. They had found a path to unity and had learned that by embracing diversity and approaching life with an open heart and mind, they could create a better world for all.

The Athlete's Journey: Applying the Gita's Principles

The Athlete's Guild was a group of elite athletes who were training to compete in the Olympic Games. They were each pursuing their own individual goals, but they shared a common commitment to excellence and a desire to reach their full potential.

As the competition approached, the athletes faced many challenges. They were under immense pressure to perform at their best, and they had to deal with injuries, setbacks, and personal struggles. It was a difficult time, and many of them felt discouraged and overwhelmed.

One day, as they were training together, one of the athletes, Rohit, suggested that they read the Bhagavad Gita. Rohit had grown up in a Hindu household and had always been drawn to the teachings of the Gita. He believed that its principles could help them to overcome their challenges and achieve their goals.

The athletes were curious but skeptical. They were focused on their training and didn't see how the Gita could help them in their athletic pursuits. However, they agreed to give it a try.

As they read the Gita, the athletes began to see the relevance of its teachings to their athletic journey. They learned about the importance of mental focus and discipline, and how to approach their training with a sense of detachment. They also learned about the importance of resilience and perseverance, and how to stay committed to their goals, even in the face of adversity.

Over time, the athletes began to apply the teachings of the Gita to their training and their competition. They found that they were able to stay more focused and disciplined, and they were able to bounce back more quickly from setbacks. They also found that they were able to approach their competition with a sense of detachment, which helped them to stay calm and focused.

As the Olympic Games approached, the athletes felt confident and prepared. They knew that they had given their all in their training, and they were ready to compete with their best efforts.

When the competition finally arrived, the Athlete's Guild performed remarkably well. They won several medals and set personal bests. But what was even more remarkable was the sense of unity and purpose that they had developed through their study of the Gita. They had formed a bond that went beyond their athletic pursuits, and they had found a path to personal growth and fulfillment.

As they reflected on their journey, the Athlete's Guild knew that the Gita had been a powerful tool for them. They had learned that by applying its principles to their athletic journey, they had found a way to overcome their challenges and reach their full potential.

The Scientist's Dilemma: Finding Guidance in the Gita

Dr. Anjali Sharma was a brilliant scientist who had devoted her life to researching advanced genetic engineering techniques. She had always been fascinated by the potential of science to transform the world, and she believed that her research had the potential to make a real difference.

However, as her research progressed, Dr. Sharma began to feel uneasy. She realized that her work had significant ethical implications, and she began to question whether she was truly acting in the best interests of humanity.

One day, as she was struggling with her doubts, a colleague suggested that she read the Bhagavad Gita. Dr. Sharma was skeptical at first, but she was willing to try anything that might help her find clarity and guidance.

As she read the Gita, Dr. Sharma found herself drawn to its teachings on ethics and responsibility. She learned about the importance of acting in accordance with dharma, or moral duty, and about the importance of considering the long-term consequences of her actions.

Over time, Dr. Sharma began to apply the teachings of the Gita to her research. She realized that she had a moral duty to use her scientific knowledge for the greater good, and she began to think more deeply about the long-term implications of her work.

As she continued to grapple with the ethical implications of her research, Dr. Sharma found that the Gita provided her with a framework for thinking about these issues. She learned to approach her work with a sense of detachment and to consider the impact of her actions on society as a whole.

In time, Dr. Sharma came to a decision about her research. She decided to focus her efforts on developing technologies that would benefit humanity, rather than those that had the potential to do harm. She was guided by the teachings of the Gita and by her sense of moral duty to act in the best interests of society.

As she continued her work, Dr. Sharma found that the Gita had given her a sense of peace and purpose. She knew that she was acting in accordance with her dharma, and that her work was making a positive contribution to the world.

In the end, Dr. Sharma's research had a significant impact on the field of genetic engineering. But what was even more significant was the way that she had approached her work. By applying the teachings of the Gita to her research, she had found a way to navigate the complex ethical issues that confronted her, and to act with a sense of responsibility and purpose.

Finding Creativity: A Musician's Journey with the Gita

Samantha was a talented musician, but she had been struggling to find inspiration for her music lately. She had been experiencing a creative block, and nothing seemed to be working. Her performances had become stale, and she felt like she was losing touch with her passion.

One day, as she was browsing through a bookstore, she came across a copy of the Bhagavad Gita. She had heard of it before but had never read it. Intrigued, she decided to give it a try.

As she began reading, Samantha was struck by the Gita's teachings on devotion and surrender. She learned about the importance of surrendering oneself to a higher power, and about the role of devotion in inspiring creativity.

Over time, Samantha began to apply these teachings to her music. She learned to let go of her ego and to surrender herself to the music, allowing it to flow through her without any resistance. She practiced devotion by dedicating herself fully to her music, putting in hours of practice each day and pouring her heart and soul into each performance.

As she began to let go of her ego and surrender herself to the music, Samantha found that her creativity began to flow freely again. She discovered new melodies and harmonies, and her performances became more powerful and moving than ever before.

Samantha's newfound devotion and surrender to her music not only reignited her creativity but also transformed her as a person. She found a deeper sense of purpose and fulfillment in her music, and her performances became a way for her to connect with something greater than herself.

In the end, Samantha's journey with the Gita had taught her a valuable lesson about the power of devotion and surrender in inspiring creativity. She knew that she would continue to apply these teachings to her music, and to her life, for years to come.

The Journey of Acceptance: Finding Guidance in the Gita

Raj and Maya had been trying to have a child for several years but had been facing infertility issues. They had tried everything, but nothing seemed to be working. The couple had been feeling hopeless and helpless, and the situation was taking a toll on their relationship.

One day, as they were going through a difficult time, a friend suggested that they read the Bhagavad Gita. Although they were not particularly religious, they were willing to try anything that might help them find peace and clarity in their situation.

As they read the Gita, Raj and Maya were struck by its teachings on acceptance and finding meaning in difficult times. They learned about the importance of accepting what is and surrendering to a higher power, and about the role of karma in shaping one's life.

Over time, the couple began to apply these teachings to their situation. They learned to accept that they may not be able to have a child and to surrender themselves to a higher power. They also began to see the situation as an opportunity to grow and to learn important life lessons.

As they continued on their journey, Raj and Maya found that the Gita had given them a sense of peace and purpose. They knew that they were acting in accordance with their dharma and that they were making the most of a difficult situation.

In the end, the couple's journey with the Gita had taught them a valuable lesson about acceptance and finding meaning in difficult times. They knew that they would continue to apply these teachings to their lives, whatever the future may hold. They also found that their journey had brought them closer together as a couple, and that they had a newfound appreciation for each other and for the journey they were on together.

The Student's Journey: Finding Purpose through the Gita

Ms. Sharma was a teacher at a high school in a rough neighborhood. Her students came from difficult backgrounds and faced many challenges in their daily lives. One of her students, Rohit, had been acting out and getting into trouble at school. Ms. Sharma knew that he was a bright student, but he seemed to be lost and without direction.

One day, as she was preparing for a class on world religions, Ms. Sharma decided to incorporate the Bhagavad Gita into the lesson. She thought that the Gita's teachings on duty, purpose, and the self would be especially relevant to her students.

As she taught the class, Ms. Sharma noticed that Rohit was particularly engaged in the discussion. He seemed to be fascinated by the Gita's teachings and asked many questions. Ms. Sharma saw an opportunity to help him find purpose and direction in his life.

Over the next few weeks, Ms. Sharma worked with Rohit, discussing the Gita's teachings and how they could be applied to his life. She encouraged him to think about his duty and his purpose, and to reflect on the nature of the self.

As Rohit began to explore these ideas, he found that he was becoming more focused and motivated. He began to see the value of hard work and dedication, and he started to apply himself more in his studies. He also began to develop a sense of purpose, as he realized that he had a duty to make a positive impact on the world.

In the end, Rohit's journey with the Gita had transformed him as a person. He had found purpose and direction in his life, and he knew that he wanted to make a difference in the world. He also had a newfound appreciation for his teacher, Ms. Sharma, who had helped him find his way.

Hope in the Storm: Finding Resilience through the Gita

The Patel family had always lived a peaceful life in their small coastal town. But one day, a massive storm hit the region, destroying their home and everything they owned. The Patel family was left with nothing but the clothes on their backs and a few personal items that they were able to save.

They were devastated and didn't know how they would recover from the disaster. But as they were trying to come to terms with their situation, a neighbor introduced them to the teachings of the Bhagavad Gita.

At first, the Patels were hesitant to explore the Gita's teachings. They were not religious, and they didn't see how a spiritual text could help them in their current situation. But their neighbor insisted, telling them that the Gita's teachings had helped her through difficult times in her life.

The Patels began to read the Gita, and they were struck by its teachings on the nature of the self and the importance of resilience. They learned about the idea of detachment and the need to focus on the things that truly matter.

As they delved deeper into the Gita's teachings, the Patels found that they were gaining strength and resilience. They began to see their situation as an opportunity to start anew and to build a better life for themselves. They learned to let go of the things that they had lost and to focus on the things that truly mattered – their family, their health, and their well-being.

With the help of the Gita's teachings, the Patels were able to find hope in the midst of their storm. They knew that they had the strength and resilience to overcome their challenges and to build a better life for themselves and their community.

Exploring the Cosmos: A Scientist's Journey with the Gita

Dr. Anika Singh was a brilliant astrophysicist who had devoted her life to understanding the mysteries of the universe. She had spent years studying the stars and galaxies, but she felt that there was something missing in her work. She was grappling with questions about the nature of the universe and the purpose of her research.

One day, a friend gave her a copy of the Bhagavad Gita, telling her that it might provide some insights into the questions she was struggling with. Dr. Singh was initially skeptical – she had never been interested in spirituality – but she decided to give the Gita a chance.

As she read the Gita, Dr. Singh was struck by its teachings on the interconnectedness of all things and the idea of a universal consciousness. She began to see her research in a new light, realizing that her work was not just about understanding the physical properties of the universe, but about uncovering the deeper truths that lay beneath the surface.

The Gita's teachings helped Dr. Singh find a sense of purpose and meaning in her work. She felt that her research was not just about discovering new things, but about uncovering the mysteries of the universe and unlocking the secrets of the cosmos.

With the Gita's guidance, Dr. Singh's work took on a new dimension. She felt a sense of awe and wonder as she gazed at the stars, knowing that they were part of a vast and interconnected web of creation. And she felt a sense of responsibility to use her knowledge for the greater good, to help others understand the beauty and complexity of the universe.

Dr. Singh's journey with the Gita taught her that the mysteries of the universe could not be fully understood through scientific inquiry alone. She realized that true understanding required a deep connection with the world around her, a connection that was rooted in the Gita's teachings of love, compassion, and service.

Finding Hope and Healing: A Journey with the Gita

Samantha, John, and Alex were lifelong friends who had grown up together in a small town. As they got older, they began to struggle with addiction and mental health challenges. They felt lost and alone, unsure of where to turn for help.

One day, Samantha stumbled upon a copy of the Bhagavad Gita at a local bookstore. She was drawn to the book's teachings on finding inner peace and overcoming challenges. She brought the book to her friends, and together they began to explore the Gita's teachings.

As they delved deeper into the Gita, Samantha, John, and Alex began to find new ways of coping with their challenges. The Gita taught them about the power of self-awareness and mindfulness, and how to cultivate a deeper connection with their inner selves.

They learned about the importance of surrendering to a higher power, and the value of faith in times of struggle. They found hope and inspiration in the Gita's teachings on overcoming obstacles and finding inner peace.

The friends began to use the Gita's teachings as a guide for their lives. They incorporated daily meditation and mindfulness practices into their routines, and began to focus on serving others in their community. They found that by helping others, they were able to find greater purpose and meaning in their own lives.

Over time, Samantha, John, and Alex's lives began to transform. They were able to overcome their addiction and mental health challenges, and found new ways of living in the world with greater joy and fulfillment. They continued to study the Gita's teachings, and found that they provided a source of comfort and guidance throughout their lives.

Their journey with the Gita showed them that healing and transformation were possible, even in the face of great adversity. They found that by embracing the Gita's teachings, they were able to connect with a deeper sense of purpose and meaning, and to find hope and healing in their lives.

Finding Hope and Healing: A Journey with the Gita

Samantha, John, and Alex were lifelong friends who had grown up together in a small town. As they got older, they began to struggle with addiction and mental health challenges. They felt lost and alone, unsure of where to turn for help.

One day, Samantha stumbled upon a copy of the Bhagavad Gita at a local bookstore. She was drawn to the book's teachings on finding inner peace and overcoming challenges. She brought the book to her friends, and together they began to explore the Gita's teachings.

As they delved deeper into the Gita, Samantha, John, and Alex began to find new ways of coping with their challenges. The Gita taught them about the power of self-awareness and mindfulness, and how to cultivate a deeper connection with their inner selves.

They learned about the importance of surrendering to a higher power, and the value of faith in times of struggle. They found hope and inspiration in the Gita's teachings on overcoming obstacles and finding inner peace.

The friends began to use the Gita's teachings as a guide for their lives. They incorporated daily meditation and mindfulness practices into their routines, and began to focus on serving others in their community. They found that by helping others, they were able to find greater purpose and meaning in their own lives.

Over time, Samantha, John, and Alex's lives began to transform. They were able to overcome their addiction and mental health challenges, and found new ways of living in the world with greater joy and fulfillment. They continued to study the Gita's teachings, and found that they provided a source of comfort and guidance throughout their lives.

Their journey with the Gita showed them that healing and transformation were possible, even in the face of great adversity. They found that by embracing the Gita's teachings, they were able to connect with a deeper sense of purpose and meaning, and to find hope and healing in their lives.

The Journey of Healing: A Young Girl's Quest for Understanding with the Bhagavad Gita

Sarika was just nine years old when her father passed away suddenly. Her world was turned upside down as she struggled to understand the loss of her beloved father. She felt lost and alone, unsure of how to move forward.

One day, Sarika's mother brought home a copy of the Bhagavad Gita, a book that Sarika's father had loved and cherished. As Sarika began to read the Gita, she found comfort in its teachings on acceptance, surrender, and the impermanence of all things in life.

The Gita taught Sarika that everything in life is temporary and that the soul is eternal. She began to understand that her father's soul still existed in some form, and that he was still with her in spirit.

As Sarika continued to study the Gita, she found new ways of coping with her grief. The Gita taught her about the power of mindfulness and meditation, and she began to practice these daily as a way of finding inner peace.

Sarika's journey with the Gita also taught her about the importance of service to others. She began volunteering in her community and found that helping others gave her a sense of purpose and joy.

As Sarika grew older, her understanding of the Gita's teachings deepened. She began to see the world with greater compassion and understanding, and found that her experiences with grief and loss had given her a unique perspective on life.

Years later, Sarika became a teacher and began to share the teachings of the Gita with her students. She found that the Gita's teachings were relevant not just to those who were grieving, but to anyone seeking greater meaning and purpose in their lives.

Through her journey with the Gita, Sarika found healing and understanding in the face of great loss. She learned that life is a journey filled with both joy and sorrow, and that by embracing the teachings of the Gita, one can find a sense of peace and purpose in the face of even the greatest challenges.

The Choice: A Young Man's Journey of Spiritual Awakening with the Bhagavad Gita

Rajat was a young man who had grown up in a wealthy family. His parents had provided him with every material comfort, and he had grown accustomed to a life of luxury and ease. However, as he entered adulthood, Rajat began to feel a deep sense of emptiness and dissatisfaction with his life. He found himself constantly searching for something more, but he didn't know what that "something" was.

One day, while browsing through a bookstore, Rajat stumbled upon a copy of the Bhagavad Gita. He had heard of the book before, but had never paid much attention to it. However, as he began to read the Gita, he found himself drawn to its teachings on selflessness, detachment, and the pursuit of spiritual fulfillment.

As he continued to study the Gita, Rajat began to realize that the pursuit of material wealth was ultimately unfulfilling, and that true happiness could only be found through a life of spiritual devotion and service to others.

However, this realization was not without its challenges. Rajat's parents and friends could not understand why he was suddenly rejecting the life of comfort and luxury they had provided him with. They saw his newfound devotion to the teachings of the Gita as a threat to their way of life, and urged him to abandon his spiritual pursuits.

Rajat found himself torn between his desire for spiritual fulfillment and his love for his family and the life he had known. But through his study of the Gita, he began to understand that the true path to happiness lay not in material possessions, but in the pursuit of inner peace and self-realization.

In the end, Rajat chose to follow the path of the Gita, and dedicated his life to spiritual service and devotion. Although his family and friends did not always understand his choices, he found great joy and fulfillment in his new way of life. He learned that the teachings of the Gita were not just words on a page, but a path to a higher consciousness and a deeper understanding of the nature of the universe.

Through his journey with the Gita, Rajat found the answers he had been searching for, and a sense of purpose and fulfillment that he had never before experienced.

The Challenge of Applying Ancient Wisdom: A Modern Take on the Gita

A group of college students enrolled in a philosophy course on the Bhagavad Gita found themselves facing a unique challenge. While they were fascinated by the ancient wisdom contained in the text, they struggled to apply its teachings to their modern lives.

As they delved deeper into the text, the students found themselves grappling with questions about the relevance of the Gita in a world that was vastly different from the one in which it was written. They wondered how they could apply its teachings on self-realization, karma, and duty to their own lives, which were filled with social media, technology, and modern social issues.

The students' professor recognized their struggle and encouraged them to think creatively about how they could apply the Gita's teachings to the modern world. She challenged them to find examples of how the Gita's principles were already being applied to contemporary issues, and to think about how they could incorporate these ideas into their own lives.

As the students worked through these challenges, they began to see the Gita in a new light. They realized that the text was not just a historical relic, but a living philosophy that could be applied to contemporary issues. They found examples of how the Gita's teachings on compassion and service were being applied to social justice issues, and how its teachings on mindfulness and inner peace were being used to address mental health challenges.

Through their study of the Gita, the students learned to think critically about how ancient wisdom could be applied to modern life. They discovered that the challenges they faced were not unique, and that the Gita's teachings could be used to guide them in their personal and professional lives.

In the end, the students emerged from the course with a newfound appreciation for the Gita and its relevance to modern life. They learned that ancient wisdom was not something to be discarded, but something to be cherished and applied to the challenges of the present day.

Overcoming Prejudice: The Gita's Teachings on Unity and Love

Maya and Raj were a young couple deeply in love, but their happiness was threatened by the discrimination they faced from their community. Maya was from a different caste than Raj, and this made them both targets of prejudice and hostility.

The couple struggled to find a way to respond to the discrimination they faced. They were angry and hurt, but they did not want to respond in kind. They wanted to find a way to stand up for themselves while remaining true to the values of compassion, love, and unity that they held dear.

One day, Maya came across a copy of the Bhagavad Gita and was struck by its teachings on karma, duty, and self-realization. She shared the text with Raj, and they began to study it together.

As they read the Gita, Maya and Raj were inspired by its teachings on the unity of all beings and the importance of treating everyone with respect and love. They were also struck by its message of selflessness and detachment, which encouraged them to focus on doing their duty without being attached to the results.

Armed with these teachings, Maya and Raj began to respond to the discrimination they faced with grace and compassion. They refused to be drawn into arguments or fights, but instead focused on showing kindness and understanding to those who were hostile to them.

Over time, their approach began to have an impact. Some people who had previously been hostile to them began to soften, and Maya and Raj were able to forge new relationships and connections within their community.

As they continued to study the Gita, Maya and Raj deepened their understanding of its teachings and their commitment to them. They saw the discrimination they faced as an opportunity to practice the Gita's message of unity and love, and to be a positive force for change in their community.

In the end, Maya and Raj's approach to the discrimination they faced was not only successful, but also deeply fulfilling. They had found a way to live in accordance with their values, and to use the teachings of the Gita to transform a difficult situation into an opportunity for growth and positive change.

Rebuilding from Within: Finding Hope in the Bhagavad Gita after a Disaster

After a devastating natural disaster, a group of survivors found themselves homeless, struggling to meet their basic needs, and mourning the loss of loved ones. They were overwhelmed with grief, fear, and uncertainty about the future.

In the midst of this crisis, a group of volunteers arrived with food, water, and medical supplies. They also brought with them copies of the Bhagavad Gita, hoping to offer comfort and guidance to the survivors.

At first, the survivors were skeptical. They had never heard of the Gita and were not sure how ancient wisdom could help them in their current situation. But as they read the text, they found a sense of calm and clarity that had been missing from their lives.

The Gita's teachings on the impermanence of material possessions, the importance of detachment, and the power of devotion resonated deeply with the survivors. They saw that the disaster had stripped away many of the things they had thought were important, and they were left with a sense of what truly mattered in life.

Using the principles of the Gita, the survivors began to rebuild their lives. They came together as a community, supporting each other through the process of rebuilding homes, businesses, and infrastructure. They focused on the present moment, finding joy in small acts of kindness and service, and cultivating a deep sense of gratitude for the simple blessings of life.

Through it all, the survivors held onto the teachings of the Gita, finding comfort and hope in its message of self-realization and the ultimate unity of all beings. They saw that the disaster had been a wake-up call, reminding them of the fragility of life and the importance of living in accordance with their deepest values.

As they emerged from the disaster, the survivors were transformed. They had found a sense of purpose and meaning in the midst of tragedy, and they carried with them the lessons of the Gita as they embarked on a new chapter of their lives.

The CEO's Dilemma: A Journey of Leadership and Responsibility

Emma had been the CEO of a large multinational corporation for several years. She had worked hard to get to where she was and had always been driven by a desire to succeed. But as her company continued to grow, she began to feel the weight of responsibility on her shoulders. She knew that the decisions she made had a ripple effect, not just on the company, but on the lives of the people it touched.

One day, Emma was faced with a difficult decision. Her company had been accused of unethical practices in its supply chain, and she had to decide how to respond. She had two options: she could deny the accusations and continue business as usual, or she could acknowledge the problem and take steps to address it.

As she grappled with this decision, Emma remembered a conversation she had had with a friend who was a spiritual teacher. They had talked about the Bhagavad Gita, and how its teachings could apply to modern life, including the challenges of leadership. Emma decided to turn to the Gita for guidance.

Emma reached out to her friend, Rohit, and asked if he could help her understand the Gita's teachings on leadership and responsibility. They set up a call, and Rohit began to explain the key principles of the text.

"Emma, the Gita teaches that as leaders, we have a duty to act with integrity and compassion," Rohit said. "We must be mindful of the impact of our actions on others, and act in a way that promotes the well-being of all."

Emma nodded, but she was still struggling to apply these principles to her current situation. "But what about when our actions conflict with the bottom line?" she asked. "What if doing the right thing puts the company at a disadvantage?"

Rohit paused for a moment, then replied. "The Gita also teaches that we must act without attachment to the results of our actions. We cannot control the outcome of our decisions, but we can control our intentions and the actions we take. If we act with integrity and compassion, the results will take care of themselves."

Emma was starting to see how the teachings of the Gita could help her in her decision-making. She thanked Rohit and promised to reflect on their conversation.

Emma continued to grapple with the decision. She consulted with her board of directors, her legal team, and her public relations department. Everyone had a different opinion, and Emma was feeling overwhelmed.

One day, she received a call from a journalist who was investigating the accusations against her company. The journalist was asking for a statement, and Emma knew she had to respond quickly.

As she sat in her office, feeling the weight of the decision, she remembered the teachings of the Gita. She closed her eyes and took a deep breath, then asked herself: What is the right thing to do?

In that moment, Emma realized that she could not deny the accusations or continue business as usual. She knew that she had a responsibility to the workers in her supply chain, and to the customers who trusted her brand. She decided to acknowledge the problem and take steps to address it.

She held a press conference, where she announced the company's commitment to ethical practices in its supply chain. She outlined a plan to work with suppliers to improve working conditions and ensure fair wages. She also announced that the company would be donating a portion of its profits to organizations that supported workers' rights.

The response was mixed. Some investors were unhappy, and the company's stock price took a temporary hit. But Emma knew that she had done the right thing. She felt a sense of clarity and purpose.

The Journey Within

Emma had always struggled with her body image and self-esteem. She spent years comparing herself to others and seeking validation from external sources. No matter what she did, she never felt good enough. It was only when she discovered the Bhagavad Gita that she began to see herself in a different light.

As Emma delved deeper into the teachings of the Gita, she realized that her worth was not determined by her appearance or the opinions of others. The Gita taught her that true happiness and fulfillment come from within, and that self-love is the foundation for a meaningful life.

Emma started to incorporate the Gita's teachings into her daily routine. She practiced meditation and yoga, which helped her connect with her inner self and develop a deeper sense of self-awareness. She also started to focus on the present moment and stopped worrying about the past or the future.

Through the Gita, Emma learned to see herself as a divine being, with unique talents and abilities. She started to appreciate her body for all that it was capable of, and stopped comparing herself to others. She realized that self-love is a journey, not a destination, and that it requires constant practice and dedication.

As Emma's self-love grew, she became more confident in all areas of her life. She pursued her passions without fear of failure, and embraced new challenges with an open mind. She formed deeper connections with others, based on mutual respect and understanding.

The Gita had transformed Emma's life in ways she never thought possible. She felt a deep sense of gratitude for the wisdom and guidance it had provided her, and she knew that it would continue to be a source of inspiration for years to come.In the end, Emma realized that the journey to self-love is not always easy, but it is always worth it.

The Gita's Guidance

A group of travelers from different parts of the world embarked on a pilgrimage to India to explore the country's rich cultural and spiritual heritage. Among them were Alex, a business executive who was looking for inner peace, and Grace, a student who wanted to understand more about spirituality. The group traveled from city to city, visiting temples and ashrams and learning about various philosophies and teachings.

One day, the group arrived at an ashram where they were introduced to the teachings of Adi Sankaracharya, a great spiritual master who lived in India more than a thousand years ago. The ashram's spiritual leader, Swamiji, explained that Adi Sankaracharya was a renowned philosopher and mystic who wrote commentaries on the Upanishads and the Bhagavad Gita, among other works.

As the travelers listened to Swamiji's talk on the Gita, they were struck by the wisdom of its teachings. Alex, who had been feeling overwhelmed and stressed by his job, was particularly drawn to the Gita's message of detachment and the importance of focusing on the present moment rather than worrying about the past or future.

Grace, who had struggled with feelings of inadequacy and self-doubt, found solace in the Gita's teachings on self-realization and the true nature of the self. She learned that the body and mind were only temporary vehicles for the soul, and that true happiness and fulfillment could only be found through connection with the divine.

As the group continued their journey, they discussed the teachings of the Gita and Adi Sankaracharya and how they could apply them to their own lives. They practiced meditation and yoga, and participated in seva, or selfless service, in the local community.

Through their experiences on the pilgrimage, the travelers learned to see the world in a new light and to approach life with greater compassion and understanding. They discovered that the Gita's teachings offered a timeless and universal path to inner peace and spiritual growth, and that anyone, regardless of their background or beliefs, could benefit from its wisdom.

In the end, the travelers returned home with a newfound sense of purpose and a deeper appreciation for the richness and diversity of the human experience.

The Entrepreneurial Journey: Applying Bhagavad Gita Principles for Success

In the bustling city of Mumbai, a group of young entrepreneurs were on a mission to revolutionize the world of business. They knew that success in business required more than just intelligence and hard work, and so they turned to the ancient Indian text, the Bhagavad Gita, for guidance.

The Bhagavad Gita, a sacred Hindu scripture, teaches that success is not just about achieving material wealth and fame, but also about cultivating a sense of purpose, service, and spiritual awareness. The entrepreneurs were inspired by these teachings and began applying them to their business practices.

One of the entrepreneurs, Ravi, had started a software development company. He had always believed that profit was the ultimate goal of business, but after reading the

Bhagavad Gita, he realized that he could use his company to serve a higher purpose. He decided to focus on developing software solutions for non-profit organizations and social enterprises, which helped him not only make a positive impact on society, but also attracted like-minded clients.

Another entrepreneur, Maya, had started a fashion brand. She had always believed that success was all about outdoing her competitors, but after studying the Bhagavad Gita, she realized that true success came from focusing on her own strengths and unique offerings. She started designing clothes that were not only fashionable, but also eco-friendly and sustainable, which set her brand apart and garnered a loyal following.

The group of entrepreneurs also applied the teachings of the Bhagavad Gita to their management style. They emphasized the importance of treating their employees with respect and kindness, and encouraged a culture of collaboration and mutual support. They also practiced mindfulness and meditation, which helped them stay grounded and focused amidst the challenges and pressures of running a business.

Their approach to business was not without its challenges, but the entrepreneurs persisted and remained committed to their principles. Over time, they found that their business practices were not only fulfilling, but also profitable. They had attracted a loyal customer base and a team of dedicated employees who shared their values and vision.

The group of entrepreneurs were now recognized as leaders in their respective industries, not just for their financial success, but also for their commitment to social impact and spiritual awareness. They had realized that true success was not just about achieving material wealth and fame, but also about making a positive impact on the world and living a purposeful life.

As they looked back on their journey, the entrepreneurs realized that the principles of the Bhagavad Gita had not only transformed their businesses, but also their lives. They had found a sense of purpose and fulfillment that went beyond their wildest dreams, and they knew that their entrepreneurial journey was only just beginning.

Finding Inner Peace: A Journey of Healing with the Bhagavad Gita

At just twenty-three years old, Meera had already faced more trauma and pain than most people experience in a lifetime. Her childhood had been marked by neglect and abuse, and she had carried those scars with her into adulthood. Despite her best efforts to move on and build a new life, Meera found herself struggling with anxiety, depression, and a sense of hopelessness.

One day, a friend recommended that Meera read the Bhagavad Gita, an ancient Indian text that contained teachings on spirituality and self-realization. Meera was skeptical at first, but as she delved into the text, she found herself drawn in by its message of hope and healing.

The teachings of the Gita spoke to Meera in a way that nothing else had before. She found comfort in the idea that all life was connected, and that the universe was guided by a higher power. She also appreciated the emphasis on self-awareness and self-realization, which encouraged her to look inward and confront the traumas and negative thought patterns that had been holding her back.

Meera began to practice meditation and mindfulness, which helped her stay present and calm in the midst of her struggles. She also started to incorporate the Gita's teachings into her daily life, focusing on the principles of detachment, non-judgment, and service. She volunteered at a local non-profit, which helped her feel a sense of purpose and connectedness.

As Meera continued on her journey of healing, she realized that the Gita had given her a framework for understanding her past and coming to terms with her experiences. She was no longer defined by her trauma, but was instead empowered by her ability to overcome it and find a sense of peace and purpose.

Meera's journey was not without its setbacks and challenges. She still experienced moments of anxiety and self-doubt, and there were times when she felt like giving up. But with the help of the Gita's teachings, she learned to persevere and trust in the universe's greater plan.

In the end, Meera emerged from her journey of healing stronger and more resilient than ever before. She had found inner peace and a sense of purpose that she had never thought possible, and she knew that the teachings of the Gita would guide her for the rest of her life.

Sustainability for a Better World: The Environmental Scientists Inspired by the Bhagavad Gita

In a world where environmental degradation was becoming more and more severe, a group of young environmental scientists were on a mission to find new solutions to help protect the planet. They knew that the traditional approaches to sustainability were not enough and they needed something more profound to guide their work. So, they turned to an unlikely source for inspiration - the Bhagavad Gita.

The Bhagavad Gita, an ancient Hindu text, emphasizes the interconnectedness of all things and the importance of living in harmony with nature. The environmental scientists found that the teachings of the Gita were directly applicable to their work and began incorporating them into their approach to sustainability.

One of the scientists, Arjun, had always believed that technology and innovation were the key to solving environmental problems. But after reading the Gita, he realized that true sustainability required a fundamental shift in human consciousness. He started to work with local communities, educating them about sustainable practices and encouraging them to take an active role in protecting the environment.

Another scientist, Radha, had always believed that the primary goal of environmentalism was to protect biodiversity. But after studying the Gita, she realized that sustainability was about more than just preserving the natural world. It was also about cultivating a sense of empathy and compassion for all living things. She started to incorporate this principle into her research, working to understand how human actions were affecting not just the environment, but also the animals and ecosystems that depend on it.

The group of scientists also found that the teachings of the Gita were relevant to their own lives. They practiced mindfulness and meditation, which helped them stay focused and connected to the natural world. They also emphasized the importance of collaboration and mutual support, recognizing that sustainability required a collective effort.

Over time, the work of the environmental scientists began to gain recognition. They had attracted the attention of government agencies, non-profit organizations, and other scientists who were inspired by their approach to sustainability. They had found that the principles of the Gita were not just theoretical, but were directly applicable to the challenges of the modern world.

As they looked back on their journey, the environmental scientists realized that the Bhagavad Gita had not only transformed their work, but also their lives. They had found a sense of purpose and fulfillment that went beyond their professional achievements, and they knew that their work was making a positive impact on the world.

In the end, the scientists were not just protecting the environment, but were also helping to build a more sustainable and compassionate world. They had found that the teachings of the Gita were not just relevant to the realm of spirituality, but were also a guide for creating a better future for all.

Navigating Ethics: A Young Lawyer's Journey with the Bhagavad Gita

Sara had always dreamed of becoming a lawyer. She believed that the justice system had the potential to make a positive impact on the world and she wanted to be a part of it. But as she began her career as a young attorney, she found that the reality of the justice system was far more complicated than she had ever imagined.

Sara was faced with ethical challenges on a daily basis. She witnessed prosecutors and defense attorneys alike bending the rules in order to secure a victory. She saw judges who were more concerned with their own careers than with upholding the law. And she struggled with the fact that sometimes, the people she was representing were guilty of the crimes they were accused of.

Sara began to feel disillusioned and wondered if the justice system was really making a positive impact on the world, or if it was just perpetuating a cycle of harm and injustice. It was then that she turned to the Bhagavad Gita, an ancient Indian text that contained teachings on morality and ethics.

The Gita spoke to Sara in a way that nothing else had before. She found comfort in the idea that there was a universal law of morality that transcended any individual's actions or intentions. She also appreciated the emphasis on selfless service and the idea that true fulfillment came from doing what was right, rather than what was expedient.

Sara began to incorporate the Gita's teachings into her approach to the law. She focused on the principles of honesty, fairness, and empathy, and sought to apply them in every case she worked on. She also started to prioritize her own well-being, practicing mindfulness and self-reflection in order to stay true to her own values.

It was not always easy for Sara to stay true to her ethical principles. She faced opposition from colleagues and clients who were more concerned with winning than with doing what was right. But with the help of the Gita's teachings, she learned to stand firm in her convictions and navigate the ethical challenges of the justice system.

As Sara continued on her journey, she found that the Gita had given her a framework for understanding her role in the world. She realized that being a lawyer was not just about winning cases, but about serving the greater good and upholding the principles of justice and morality.

In the end, Sara emerged from her journey with a renewed sense of purpose and a commitment to making a positive impact on the world. She knew that the teachings of the Gita would guide her in all aspects of her life, and that she had found a deeper meaning in her work as a lawyer.

Compassionate Care: Nurses and the Bhagavad Gita

In a busy hospital in a large city, a group of nurses were faced with the daily challenge of caring for patients who were sick, in pain, and often scared. They worked long hours, dealing with difficult cases and challenging family members. The pressure to perform their duties flawlessly, with no mistakes, was overwhelming.

The nurses, however, were drawn to the principles of the Bhagavad Gita. They believed that the teachings of the Gita could help them provide better care for their patients while remaining emotionally detached. They began meeting regularly to discuss the Gita and to apply its principles to their work.

One of the key principles they learned from the Gita was detachment. They were taught that detachment was essential for good decision-making and for keeping an objective view. They realized that, by detaching themselves from the emotional challenges of their work, they could provide better care and make more effective decisions for their patients.

Another principle they applied was the concept of Karma Yoga. Karma Yoga teaches the importance of doing one's duty without seeking personal gain. The nurses realized that they were in their profession to serve others and that they needed to put the well-being of their patients first, even if it meant making sacrifices.

The nurses found that by applying these principles, they could approach each patient with compassion and detachment, which helped them stay calm and focused. They were able to connect with their patients in a way that was more meaningful and less clinical, which made their patients feel seen and valued.

As they continued to apply the teachings of the Gita, the nurses also found that they were taking better care of themselves. They practiced self-care, such as meditation and journaling, which helped them stay grounded and centered in the face of the challenges of their work.

Their patients noticed the difference in their approach, and the hospital administration took notice as well. The nurses were recognized for their compassionate care and were praised for their ability to remain calm and objective in even the most difficult situations.

The nurses were grateful for the guidance of the Bhagavad Gita, which had helped them in their work and in their personal lives. They knew that the principles they had learned would continue to guide them as they worked to care for their patients with compassion and detachment, even in the face of adversity.

The Path of Acceptance: A Journey Through Fertility with the Bhagavad Gita

Maya had always dreamed of having a family, but after years of trying to conceive, she was diagnosed with infertility. Her dreams were shattered, and she felt lost and hopeless. She didn't know how to move forward or how to find peace with her situation.

Desperate for answers, Maya turned to the Bhagavad Gita. She had heard that the teachings of the Gita could provide a path to acceptance and hope, even in the face of difficult challenges. Maya had never been particularly religious, but she was willing to try anything that might bring her peace.

Maya learned that the Gita teaches that detachment is essential for inner peace. She realized that she needed to detach herself from the outcome of her efforts to conceive and focus on the present moment. She began to practice meditation and mindfulness, which helped her to stay present and let go of her worries about the future.

Another principle that Maya found helpful was the idea of surrender. The Gita teaches that one must surrender to a higher power and trust that everything will work out in the end. Maya found this idea difficult to grasp at first, but with time, she began to let go of her need for control and trust that the universe had a plan for her.

Maya also found comfort in the concept of karma. She realized that she had done everything she could to try to conceive, and now she needed to trust that the outcome was beyond her control. Maya believed that if she continued to do good in the world, she would be rewarded in some way, even if it wasn't through having a child.

As Maya continued to apply the teachings of the Gita to her life, she found that her outlook began to shift. She no longer felt overwhelmed by her situation but instead felt a sense of peace and acceptance. She knew that her journey was not over and that there would still be challenges ahead, but she was ready to face them with a newfound sense of hope and courage.

Maya learned that the Gita's teachings provided a way to find acceptance and hope in even the most difficult circumstances. She was grateful for the wisdom of the Gita, which had helped her through her journey, and knew that it would continue to guide her in the future.

The Power of Mindfulness: An Exploration of the Bhagavad Gita's Teachings

A group of researchers at a prominent university were studying the effects of mindfulness and meditation on the brain. They had spent years examining brain scans and conducting experiments to understand the benefits of these practices. However, they felt that something was missing. They wanted to gain a deeper understanding of the philosophy behind these practices and how they related to the human experience.

One day, one of the researchers came across the Bhagavad Gita, a Hindu text that espouses the power of meditation, mindfulness, and detachment. The group was fascinated by the wisdom contained in the text and decided to incorporate it into their research.

They began to explore the Gita's teachings on detachment and how it related to the practice of mindfulness. They learned that detachment meant not being attached to the outcomes of our actions and that mindfulness involved being present and aware of the present moment without judgment.

The researchers found that these teachings could be applied to their work on mindfulness and meditation. They began to incorporate the principles of detachment and mindfulness into their research and found that it brought a new level of understanding to their work. They discovered that the Gita's teachings were not only relevant to ancient times but also had practical applications in modern-day research.

As they continued to delve into the text, the researchers found that the Gita also taught about the power of the mind and the importance of self-awareness. They began to see how these teachings could be applied to their work and how they could help people to live more fulfilling and meaningful lives.

The researchers felt that the Gita had provided them with a new perspective on mindfulness and meditation. They realized that these practices were not just about relaxation and stress reduction but could also bring a deeper sense of understanding and wisdom to people's lives.

In the end, the researchers were grateful for the wisdom and insight that the Gita had provided them. They knew that their research would never be the same and that they had been given a new lens through which to view their work. They hoped that their findings would be able to help people to live more fulfilling and mindful lives.

The Yoga of the Bhagavad Gita: Finding Spiritual Awareness

In a small yoga community nestled in the foothills of the Himalayas, a group of practitioners came together to deepen their understanding of the practice. They had been practicing for many years, but they felt that something was missing. They wanted to connect their practice to something greater, to find a deeper meaning and purpose.

One day, one of the practitioners came across the Bhagavad Gita, a Hindu text that is revered as a spiritual guide. They were immediately drawn to the wisdom contained in the text and decided to incorporate it into their practice.

They began to study the Gita's teachings on yoga, which describe it as a way of life that encompasses physical, mental, and spiritual practices. They learned that the ultimate goal of yoga is to connect with the divine, and that the path to achieving this goal involves the cultivation of certain virtues such as selflessness, humility, and detachment.

The practitioners found that these teachings provided a new level of depth to their practice. They began to see how the physical postures, breathing techniques, and meditation practices they had been doing for years were all part of a larger spiritual journey.

As they continued to study the Gita, they found that it also provided guidance on how to live a meaningful and purposeful life. They learned about the importance of acting selflessly and doing one's duty without being attached to the outcomes. They also discovered the power of surrendering to a higher power and trusting in the divine plan.

The group began to apply these teachings to their daily lives and found that they brought a new level of peace, purpose, and fulfillment. They became more compassionate, patient, and understanding of others, and found greater meaning in their work and relationships.

The practitioners also began to share their newfound knowledge with others, offering workshops and classes on the yoga of the Gita. They found that many people were drawn to the teachings and that they provided a fresh perspective on yoga and spirituality.

In the end, the group was grateful for the wisdom and insight that the Gita had provided them. They knew that their practice would never be the same and that they had been given a new lens through which to view their lives. They hoped that their findings would inspire others to deepen their practice and find greater spiritual awareness.

The Balance of Duty and Self-Care: A Woman's Journey with the Bhagavad Gita

Anjali was a successful lawyer, driven and ambitious. She worked long hours, often well into the night, and felt proud of her accomplishments. But she also had a family, a husband and two young children who needed her attention and love.

As her workload increased, Anjali found it increasingly difficult to balance the demands of her career with the needs of her family. She was constantly torn between her responsibilities at work and her responsibilities at home, and felt guilty no matter where she turned.

One day, she came across the Bhagavad Gita, a text that she had heard of but never read. As she delved into the teachings of the Gita, she found that it provided her with a new perspective on her life.

She learned that one's duty is not just to oneself, but to the world around them. She also learned about the importance of self-care and balance, and how one must take care of oneself in order to effectively care for others.

As she continued to study the Gita, she found that it provided a framework for her to balance her responsibilities at work with her responsibilities at home. She learned about the importance of detachment, of doing one's duty without being attached to the outcome. She also learned about the importance of self-awareness and mindfulness, and how these practices could help her to stay grounded and centered in the midst of her busy life.

Anjali began to apply these teachings to her daily life, and found that they brought a new level of peace and balance to her life. She began to prioritize self-care and set boundaries at work, so that she could be fully present with her family when she was at home. She also found that she was able to approach her work with a new sense of detachment, which allowed her to be more effective and less stressed.

Over time, Anjali found that she had created a new balance in her life, one that allowed her to pursue her career goals while also being there for her family. She knew that it would never be perfect, but she was grateful for the wisdom and insight that the Gita had provided her. She hoped that her experience would inspire others to find their own balance of duty and self-care, and to live a life that is both meaningful and fulfilling.

Embracing Impermanence: A Journey with the Bhagavad Gita

Raj was a young man with a bright future ahead of him. He had a successful career, loving family, and many friends. Yet despite all his blessings, he had a deep-seated fear of death that plagued him day and night.

He tried everything to shake this fear. He consulted doctors, therapists, and spiritual gurus, but nothing seemed to help. He was constantly consumed by the thought of his own mortality and the fragility of life.

One day, Raj stumbled upon the Bhagavad Gita, an ancient text that he had never heard of before. As he read through its teachings, he found that it spoke directly to his fears and anxieties. The Gita taught him that everything in life is impermanent, and that death is a natural part of the cycle of existence.

At first, this idea was terrifying to Raj. But as he continued to study the Gita, he found that its teachings brought him a sense of peace and acceptance that he had never felt before. He learned about the importance of living in the present moment, and of cherishing each and every day that he was given.

He also learned about the power of surrender, of releasing his attachment to outcomes and trusting in the greater plan of the universe. As he began to apply these teachings to his daily life, he found that his fear of death began to recede.

Over time, Raj developed a new perspective on life, one that was rooted in the impermanence of all things. He began to see the beauty and wonder in the fleeting moments of life, and he learned to appreciate every experience, no matter how small or ordinary. He found that he could now live with a sense of gratitude and joy, even in the face of his own mortality.

Raj knew that his journey was far from over, but he was grateful for the wisdom and insight that the Gita had provided him. He hoped that his experience would inspire others to embrace the impermanence of life, and to find comfort in the knowledge that everything is a part of a larger, more meaningful whole.

Adi Shankaracharya: The Philosopher Who Influenced Hindu Thought

Adi Shankaracharya, also known as Shankara Bhagavatpada, was a philosopher and theologian who lived in India in the eighth century CE. He is widely regarded as one of the most important figures in the development of Hindu philosophy, and his teachings continue to influence spiritual thought and practice to this day.

Early Life and Education

Adi Shankaracharya was born in 788 CE in a village called Kaladi, in the present-day state of Kerala in India. His parents were devout Hindus who raised him in the traditions of their faith. As a child, he showed a remarkable aptitude for learning and an interest in spirituality.

At the age of eight, Adi Shankaracharya became a disciple of a renowned teacher named Govinda Bhagavatpada. Under his guidance, Shankara studied the Vedas, the Upanishads, and other sacred texts of the Hindu tradition. He quickly mastered these texts and became known for his extraordinary intellect and insight.

Teachings

Adi Shankaracharya's teachings are rooted in the Advaita Vedanta, a school of Hindu philosophy that emphasizes the non-dual nature of reality. According to this philosophy, the true nature of the self is identical to the ultimate reality of the universe, which is often referred to as Brahman.

One of the key teachings of Advaita Vedanta is the concept of maya, or illusion. According to Shankara, maya is the cause of our perception of separation and duality in the world. It is the result of the limited perception of the human mind, which sees only a small part of the larger whole.

To overcome maya, Shankara taught the practice of jnana yoga, or the yoga of knowledge. This involves cultivating self-knowledge through the study of sacred texts and reflection on their teachings. Through this practice, one can come to realize the non-dual nature of reality and the true nature of the self.

Shankara also emphasized the importance of devotion to a personal deity, such as Shiva or Vishnu. He believed that devotion could lead to a deepening of spiritual awareness and a more profound experience of the divine.

Legacy

Adi Shankaracharya's influence on Hindu thought and practice cannot be overstated. His teachings have inspired countless spiritual seekers and scholars throughout the centuries, and his philosophy continues to be studied and debated to this day.

In addition to his philosophical contributions, Shankara also founded four monasteries, or mathas, in different parts of India. These institutions continue to play a vital role in the preservation and propagation of Hindu philosophy and culture.

Sripad Ramanujacharya: The Philosopher Who Shaped Vaishnavism

Sripad Ramanujacharya, also known as Ramanuja, was a philosopher and theologian who lived in India during the eleventh and twelfth centuries CE. He is widely regarded as one of the most important figures in the development of

Vaishnavism, a tradition within Hinduism that emphasizes devotion to the god Vishnu and his incarnations.

Early Life and Education

Sripad Ramanujacharya was born in 1017 CE in a village called Sriperumbudur, in the present-day state of Tamil Nadu in India. His parents were devout Hindus who raised him in the traditions of their faith. As a child, he showed a remarkable aptitude for learning and an interest in spirituality.

At the age of sixteen, Ramanuja became a disciple of a renowned teacher named Yadava Prakasha. Under his guidance, Ramanuja studied the Vedas, the Upanishads, and other sacred texts of the Hindu tradition. He quickly mastered these texts and became known for his extraordinary intellect and insight.

Teachings

Ramanuja's teachings are rooted in the philosophy of Vishishtadvaita, a school of Hindu thought that emphasizes the qualified non-dual nature of reality. According to this philosophy, while ultimate reality is non-dual, it is also qualified by the attributes of God, such as love, mercy, and compassion.

One of Ramanuja's key contributions to Vaishnavism was his emphasis on the importance of devotion to God. He taught that devotion could lead to a deepening of spiritual awareness and a more profound experience of the divine. He also emphasized the importance of community and social service, believing that these were essential aspects of the spiritual life.

Ramanuja is perhaps best known for his commentary on the Brahma Sutras, a foundational text of Hindu philosophy. In this commentary, he presents a detailed exposition of his philosophy of Vishishtadvaita, drawing on the teachings of the Upanishads and other sacred texts.

Legacy

Sripad Ramanujacharya's influence on Vaishnavism and Hindu thought more broadly cannot be overstated. His teachings have inspired countless spiritual seekers and scholars throughout the centuries, and his philosophy continues to be studied and debated to this day.

In addition to his philosophical contributions, Ramanuja also founded several monasteries and temples throughout southern India. These institutions continue to play a vital role in the preservation and propagation of Vaishnava philosophy and culture.

Sripad Madhavacharya: The Philosopher Who Established Dvaita Vedanta

Sripad Madhavacharya, also known as Madhvacharya or Ananda Tirtha, was a philosopher and theologian who lived in India during the thirteenth century CE. He is widely regarded as one of the most important figures in the development of Dvaita Vedanta, a school of Hindu thought that emphasizes the eternal distinction between God and the individual soul.

Early Life and Education

Madhavacharya was born in 1238 CE in a village called Pajaka, in the present-day state of Karnataka in India. His parents were devout Hindus who raised him in the traditions of their faith. As a child, he showed a remarkable aptitude for learning and an interest in spirituality.

At the age of twelve, Madhavacharya left home to study with a renowned teacher named Achyutapreksha. Under his guidance, Madhavacharya studied the Vedas, the Upanishads, and other sacred texts of the Hindu tradition. He quickly mastered these texts and became known for his extraordinary intellect and insight.

Teachings

Madhavacharya's teachings are rooted in the philosophy of Dvaita Vedanta, which emphasizes the eternal distinction between God and the individual soul. According to this philosophy, while God is the supreme reality, the individual soul is also real, distinct, and eternal.

One of Madhavacharya's key contributions to Dvaita Vedanta was his emphasis on the importance of devotion to God. He taught that devotion could lead to a deepening of spiritual awareness and a more profound experience of the divine. He also emphasized the importance of ethical conduct and social service, believing that these were essential aspects of the spiritual life.

Madhavacharya is perhaps best known for his commentary on the Brahma Sutras, a foundational text of Hindu philosophy. In this commentary, he presents a detailed exposition of his philosophy of Dvaita Vedanta, drawing on the teachings of the Upanishads and other sacred texts.

Legacy

Sripad Madhavacharya's influence on Dvaita Vedanta and Hindu thought more broadly cannot be overstated. His teachings have inspired countless spiritual seekers and scholars throughout the centuries, and his philosophy continues to be studied and debated to this day.

In addition to his philosophical contributions, Madhavacharya also founded several monasteries and temples throughout southern India. These institutions continue to play a vital role in the preservation and propagation of Dvaita Vedanta philosophy and culture.

Shri Ramakrishna Paramhamsa: Life and Teachings of a Great Spiritual Master

Shri Ramakrishna Paramhamsa was a 19th-century Indian mystic and spiritual teacher who inspired a spiritual renaissance in India and around the world. He was born in a small village in West Bengal in 1836, and from a young age, he showed a deep interest in religion and spirituality. He spent much of his early life in search of a true spiritual teacher, and eventually, he found his guru in the form of the goddess Kali, whom he saw as the embodiment of the divine mother.

Ramakrishna's spiritual experiences were intense and often ecstatic, and he soon became known as a great spiritual master. He taught a universal message of love and devotion, which he saw as the essence of all religions. He had many disciples, including the great Indian saint Swami Vivekananda, who would go on to spread his teachings around the world.

Ramakrishna's teachings emphasized the importance of direct experience of the divine, which he called "God realization." He believed that there are many paths to God, and that all religions lead to the same ultimate reality. He encouraged his disciples to practice spiritual disciplines like prayer, meditation, and devotion to God, and he taught that it is possible to achieve enlightenment in this very life.

Ramakrishna's life and teachings have had a profound impact on the spiritual landscape of India and the world. His message of love and devotion has inspired millions of people to seek a deeper understanding of the divine, and his legacy continues to inspire spiritual seekers to this day.

Shri Chaitanya Mahaprabhu: Life and Teachings of the Father of the Bhakti Movement

Shri Chaitanya Mahaprabhu was a 16th-century Indian saint and spiritual master who is known as the father of the Bhakti movement. He was born in Bengal in 1486, and from a young age, he showed a deep interest in spiritual matters. As a young man, he became a devotee of Lord Krishna, and he soon began to preach the message of love and devotion to God.

Chaitanya's teachings emphasized the importance of devotion, or bhakti, as the path to God realization. He taught that through chanting the names of God and engaging in devotional practices like singing and dancing, one can experience the divine presence within oneself. He believed that all living beings are eternal servants of God, and that by surrendering to the will of God, one can achieve spiritual liberation.

Chaitanya's life was marked by deep devotion and intense spiritual experiences. He attracted many followers, who were inspired by his message of love and devotion to God. He traveled throughout India, preaching and teaching, and his teachings had a profound impact on the spiritual landscape of the country.

Today, Chaitanya's legacy continues to inspire millions of people around the world. His message of love and devotion to God has helped to transform the lives of countless individuals, and his teachings continue to be a source of guidance and inspiration for spiritual seekers everywhere.

As we come to the end of this book, we hope that the stories within have offered you a glimpse into the profound wisdom and teachings of the Bhagavad Gita. The Gita is not merely a text to be studied, but a path to be walked, a journey of self-discovery and inner transformation that requires courage, dedication, and perseverance.

Each story in this book is intended to serve as a stepping stone on that path, offering insights and guidance that can help us navigate the challenges and opportunities of our lives with greater awareness, compassion, and wisdom. Whether we are facing difficult choices, struggling with inner conflicts, or simply seeking to deepen our understanding of ourselves and the world around us, the teachings of the Gita can offer us a source of strength and guidance.

We hope that the stories in this book have inspired you to explore the wisdom of the Gita for yourself, to delve deeper into the timeless teachings of this beloved text, and to continue on the path of self-discovery and spiritual transformation.

We would like to express our deepest gratitude to the author, Sourish Dutta, for bringing this book to life, and for sharing his wisdom and insights with the world. We would also like to thank our readers for joining us on this journey of discovery and learning, and for their dedication to the path of self-realization and inner peace.

May the teachings of the Bhagavad Gita continue to guide us all towards a more compassionate, loving, and enlightened world.

Om Shanti, Shanti, Shanti.

Soma Pal and Madhushree Ghosh